D1505853

Journey to Freedom

MARY MCLEOD BETHUNE

BY AMY ROBIN JONES

"I WOULD NOT EXCHANGE MY COLOR
FOR ALL THE WEALTH IN THE WORLD,
FOR HAD I BEEN BORN WHITE I MIGHT
NOT HAVE BEEN ABLE TO DO ALL THAT I
HAVE DONE OR YET HOPE TO DO."
— MARY MCLEOD BETHUNE —

Cover and page 4 caption:
A portrait of Mary McLeod
Bethune around 1943

Content Consultants:
Staff at the Mary McLeod
Bethune National Historic Site

Published in the United States of America by The Child's World®
1980 Lookout Drive, Mankato, MN 56003-1705
800-599-READ • www.childsworld.com

ACKNOWLEDGEMENTS

The Child's World®: Mary Berendes, Publishing Director

The Design Lab: Kathleen Petelinsek, Design; Gregory Lindholm, Page Production

Red Line Editorial: Holly Saari, Editorial Direction

PHOTOS

Cover and page 4: Harrison Studio/NPS/Mary McLeod Bethune Council House
National Historic Site

Interior: AP Images, 7, 17; Bethune-Cookman University archives, 6, 8, 11; Bettmann/Corbis, 13,
16, 20, 22, 23, 26; Corbis, 14, 19, 24, 25; Gordon Parks/Corbis, 12; NPS/Mary McLeod Bethune
Council House National Historic Site, 27; Schomburg Center for Research in Black Culture/New
York Public Library archives, 5

LIBRARY OF CONGRESS CATALOGING-IN-PUBLICATION DATA

Jones, Amy Robin, 1958–

  Mary McLeod Bethune / by Amy Robin Jones.

    p. cm. — (Journey to freedom)

  Includes bibliographical references and index.

  ISBN 978-1-60253-129-1 (library bound : alk. paper)

 1. Bethune, Mary McLeod, 1875–1955—Juvenile literature. 2. African American women—
Biography—Juvenile literature. 3. African Americans—Biography—Juvenile literature. 4.
Teachers—United States—Juvenile literature. 5. African American women civil rights workers—
Biography—Juvenile literature. I. Title. II. Series.

E185.97.B34J66 2009

370.92—dc22

[B]

                                    2008031934

CONTENTS

Mary McLeod Bethune was a leader in improving education for blacks.

Chapter One

SEEKING AND SHARING EDUCATION

ary McLeod Bethune looked around. A small shack stood in the middle of what was once a garbage dump. Bits of rubbish poked out of the ground. Pine and oak trees baked in the hot sun. Bethune looked past this and envisioned something more. She pictured a large white building surrounded by gardens. She imagined young girls walking on sidewalks. She saw students and teachers.

A few years earlier, in 1904, Bethune had started a small school for black girls in Daytona Beach, Florida. It began with only five students. It was now 1907, and her plan was to expand the school. She needed more land to do so.

"It's $250," said Mr. Kinsey, the landowner, halting Bethune's thoughts. She looked at him. Then she looked around the abandoned field once more. She smiled and said, "I'll bring you a down payment."

Bethune did not have the money for the down payment. When she got home, she went straight to her kitchen. She baked all day and night so she could sell the items to raise money. Bethune asked friends and students to help her. She went to everyone she knew explaining her dream of moving her small school from a four-room cottage to a large school grounds with many buildings. By the end of the week, Bethune had the down payment for the land—five dollars. She wrapped up the money in a handkerchief and brought it to Kinsey. Bethune now owned land for her new school.

Mary McLeod Bethune took great strides toward improving education for blacks. She was the first black woman to start a college for black students and the first black woman to be president of a college. Bethune dedicated her life to improving the lives of black people.

Old Faith Hall was one of the first major structures built for Bethune's school, the Daytona Normal and Industrial Institute.

Similar to this family, the McLeod family picked cotton on their farm to make a living.

Chapter Two

DREAMS AND DETERMINATION

ary Jane McLeod was born on July 10, 1875, in Mayesville, South Carolina. Her parents were Samuel and Patsy McLeod. Mary was the fifteenth of seventeen children. The U.S. Civil War had ended ten years earlier, freeing Mary's parents and several of her older siblings from slavery.

The McLeod family worked on their five-acre (2-ha) farm growing cotton. Life was difficult in the South for freed slaves. The McLeods grew their own food and made almost everything they needed. Growing up, Mary worked hard to help her family. She once boasted that at nine years old she could pick 250 pounds (113 kg) of cotton in one day.

Mary McLeod Bethune was born and raised in this wooden cabin in Mayesville, South Carolina.

Slavery in the United States lasted for almost 250 years. It began in 1619 at the first colony of Jamestown, now located in Virginia. Slavery finally ended with the Thirteenth **Amendment** to the U.S. Constitution in 1865.

There was little time for Mary or her siblings to go to school. Even if there had been time, few black children had the opportunity for a public education. Because of **segregation**, black children in the South were not allowed to attend classes with white children. It was legal to segregate whites and blacks in public places, such as schools, churches, and theaters. Many whites did not want blacks to be educated. There were not many schools that black children could attend.

8

Even so, Mary's mother and father wanted at least one of their children to receive an education. In 1885, Mary's parents chose her to attend Trinity Presbyterian Mission School. It was a school for black children. Ten-year-old Mary awoke early each morning, did her chores, and then walked to school. She studied hard during classes, walked home, and did more chores. Then each night, she taught her brothers and sisters what she had learned that day.

Mary did well in school. In 1887, when she was 12, Mary's teachers selected her to receive a **scholarship** to attend the Scotia **Seminary** in Concord, North Carolina. At the seminary, Mary received religious training and an industrial education. This provided her with skills to find work in sewing, cooking, washing, and cleaning. Mary also excelled in English and learned to speak and write with confidence.

After Mary completed her education at the Scotia Seminary in 1894, she attended Moody Bible Institute in Chicago, Illinois. Moody Institute sent **missionaries** to countries around the world. Mary wanted to become a missionary in Africa, where her mother was born. But Moody Institute would not send a black missionary to Africa. Mary's goals turned elsewhere.

She began teaching at the Haines Institute in Augusta, Georgia. At the Institute, Mary found a love of teaching. She decided that her life's mission would be to help black children receive an education.

In Bethune's time, segregation wasn't the only difficulty black people faced. They also had a hard time voting because some whites threatened them when they tried to register. Poll taxes and voter registration "tests" were used to prevent black people from voting.

Mary knew that black students received a very limited education compared to whites. Generally, schools for black students only offered classes to help them become better servants or laborers. They did not teach students how to be leaders. Mary realized that girls were rarely included in education plans. She intended to change that. Black girls would not only learn the skills to find work, but they would also gain the knowledge to improve their lives.

While teaching at Haines Institute, Mary met a fellow teacher named Albertus Bethune. In May of 1898, the two married. In February of 1899, Mary gave birth to a son, Albert McLeod Bethune.

In 1899, the family moved to Florida, where Albertus had found a job. It was there that Mary would fulfill her dream of establishing her own school. In 1904, she opened the Daytona Educational and Industrial Training School for Negro Girls in Daytona Beach, Florida. Her first class was made up of only five young girls. Their parents paid **tuition** of 50 cents each week. Soon four-year-old Albert attended the school too. When area parents discovered that Mary taught girls, her school quickly grew.

By 1907, Mary and her husband had separated. Mary continued to teach and to develop her school. She worked hard to raise money for it. Both blacks and whites of Daytona Beach offered to help. They donated money, books, and furniture.

In 1923, Bethune's school merged with Cookman Institute for Negro Boys in Jacksonville, Florida, to become a high school. In 1929, the combined school was renamed Bethune-Cookman College. In 2007, the college became a university, and the name changed to Bethune-Cookman University.

Mary McLeod Bethune (in front of fence) standing with students assembled at the Daytona Normal and Industrial Institute

While her educational mission was underway, Mary realized another area that needed her help—medical care for blacks. The Daytona Beach hospital was segregated. Mary wanted to make sure blacks received good medical care, just as whites did. In 1911, she opened a new hospital next to her school. Both black and white doctors worked at the McLeod Hospital, and all patients were treated equally.

Students in their dormitory at Bethune-Cookman College in 1943

Chapter Three

THE WOMAN'S ERA

n 1920, women in the United States gained the right to vote, but equality did not come with it. Men were welcome in the workforce, but women were not. Bethune became active in working toward women's equality. She believed that women could not achieve their **potential** because of limited opportunities. Bethune believed women could do more with their lives if they had the same opportunities as men.

In addition to her work in education, Bethune found time to work with other groups—especially those that helped women and blacks. She strongly believed that black women could make a difference in the world around them. They just needed to

Mary McLeod Bethune worked tirelessly for the causes she believed in.

cooperate and work together. She joined forces with other women who had the same ideas.

Bethune and many women like her believed that they should be able to do more than work in their homes and care for their families. They could handle other responsibilities. Black women could work to improve the lives of others in their communities. The period from around 1890 to 1940 has been called the "Woman's Era" in black history. Black women from all over the country started establishing and joining groups dedicated to improving the lives of others in their communities.

In 1921, Bethune joined a group called the National Association of Wage Earners (NAWE). One goal of the NAWE was to educate working black women. Black workers were usually paid less than white workers. Sometimes, employers fired blacks because of **prejudice**. Black workers were often given too much work to do in a single day. The NAWE believed black women deserved better wages and working conditions. The group taught working women to fight for fair treatment.

Bethune also joined the National Association of Colored Women's Clubs (NACWC). This group strived to improve women's lives. It worked to end **racism**, **sexism**, and **discrimination**. The NACWC was also one of the first groups to help support Bethune's school.

By 1924, the NACWC had more than 10,000 members. By this time, other members knew Bethune was energetic, powerful, and intelligent. She was also a gifted speaker and writer. When Bethune spoke to people, she could move and inspire them. That year, Bethune was voted president of the NACWC. She served as the organization's president until 1928.

Still, U.S. segregation laws continued to discriminate against blacks in many places. By law, blacks could not use the same public facilities as whites. Bethune refused to accept this. She not only made people aware of the unfair laws and **policies**, but she also worked hard to change them.

In 1927, Bethune attended a meeting of the National Council of Women (NCW). The NCW was a segregated organization with mostly white, female members. The event was held at the home of Franklin Delano Roosevelt, who was the governor of New York at the time. His wife, Eleanor Roosevelt, was hosting.

Bethune was the eighth president of the NACWC. One of her largest accomplishments in this role was establishing a national headquarters for the organization in Washington DC.

At the NCW meeting, a white woman told Bethune it was wonderful for Mrs. Roosevelt to have her at the meeting. The woman pointed out that Bethune was the only black person there. Bethune spoke to her with humor. She told the woman it was nice of Mrs. Roosevelt to have everyone at her home.

There was a moment of silence when Bethune entered the Roosevelts' home. Bethune was tall, confident, and intelligent. Still, many of the white women in the NCW were prejudiced. The Roosevelts were not. Sara Delano Roosevelt, Franklin's mother, took Bethune by the arm. The two women sat next to each other. Like Bethune, the Roosevelt family stood up against racism in whatever way they could. Bethune and Eleanor Roosevelt became close friends. They were partners in the struggle for racial equality.

Eleanor Roosevelt and Mary McLeod Bethune at the 1939 National Conference on Problems of the Negro and Negro Youth

President Franklin Roosevelt in 1933

Chapter Four

A TIME OF TURMOIL

ethune had been working with the NACWC for some time but was not satisfied with the organization. Members in different states did not communicate very well with each other. In 1935, Bethune founded the National Council of Negro Women (NCNW). The council was an organization of organizations. Existing organizations would join the NCNW. The NCNW would then help track all the organizations' activities. Bethune still had a vision of what black women could accomplish if they worked together. She hoped the NCNW would be a way to achieve this vision.

As a recipient of the *Spingarn Medal, Bethune is among several blacks who were recognized for their hard work for equality and **civil rights**. Other well-known recipients include W. E. B. Du Bois, Martin Luther King Jr., and Rosa Parks.*

That same year, Bethune's hard work was rewarded when she received the Spingarn Medal. The National Association for the Advancement of Colored People (NAACP) awards this honor each year to a black person for outstanding achievement. Bethune was honored for her work as the founder and president of Bethune-Cookman College and her national leadership in black equality.

Shortly after this award, Bethune was given another honor. Franklin D. Roosevelt became president of the United States in 1933. He had met Bethune through his wife, Eleanor, and admired her work. In 1935, he asked Bethune to work with him as an advisor on Negro affairs. She served as President Roosevelt's advisor from 1936 to 1943.

Bethune had a lot of work to do in her new position. The **Great Depression** that began with a drought in the late 1920s and the stock market crash of 1929 gripped the United States. Many people lost their jobs and could not find work. Thousands of people were without homes. The Great Depression may have been worse for black people than for whites. Many government agencies that helped those in need had racist policies. Blacks were often discriminated against. Jobs were found for white workers first. Money was given to white people first. Blacks received what was left over, which was often nothing. Bethune worked to change these practices.

Although Bethune was an important U.S. leader, she still faced racism. People called her rude names. They tried to make her feel inferior, but she would not give in. One evening, Bethune was leaving an event at the White House. A southern politician asked her, "Auntie, what are you doing here?" "Auntie" was an offensive term some white Southerners called older black, female servants. She looked at him and said, "Why, how do you do. Now which one of my sisters' children are you?" Even when she was angry, Bethune used her sense of humor to make a point.

Bethune believed the best way to fight racism was with intelligence. She began to make a difference through her work with President Roosevelt. She helped develop the president's policies on race and discrimination. She worked with the National Youth Administration (NYA), a U.S. government group that helped youths find jobs. As a result of Bethune's actions, the NYA adopted nondiscrimination policies.

Bethune had a strong interest in youth development and was still active in improving black education. She believed that black

Some National Youth Administration (NYA) women worked in beauty shops.

students needed better schools and more places to go for recreation. Bethune worked closely with the NYA to establish funding for black schools.

Because of Bethune's success with the NYA, President Roosevelt named her the director of the NYA's Division of Negro Affairs in 1936. Through this role, she started special programs for black youth. She also encouraged the government to continue to aid black students' tuition for schooling.

Bethune's accomplishments in her role in government were great. Because of her efforts, black reporters were finally admitted to the White House for news meetings. Bethune demanded that black doctors be allowed to work at Johns Hopkins Hospital in Maryland. Black nurses were finally allowed to work at Freedmen's Hospital in Washington DC.

Bethune also helped organize the Federal Council on Negro Affairs. This group recruited black advisors into the government. The council held two conferences, the first in 1937 and the

Mary McLeod Bethune greeted these new members into the Women's Army Corps.

second in 1939. Bethune was in charge of both. When arguments arose, Bethune used her strength and faith to regain order. She would say, "Let's now have prayer." The room would grow quiet as her voice rose in a hymn. Faith played an important role in Bethune's life. Her religious beliefs helped give her the confidence and strength needed to lead others.

As Bethune worked to solve problems in her own country, problems outside the United States were growing. Many parts of the world were changing. Europe was at war. It looked as if the United States would soon become involved.

In 1941, the United States entered the war after Japan bombed the U.S. Naval Fleet at Pearl Harbor in the U.S. territory of Hawaii. During World War II (1939–1945), the NYA organized a program to train pilots. Bethune made sure that six black colleges offered the program to students. After their training, black pilots were able to fly military airplanes.

Thousands of blacks fought to protect their country, but they were treated unfairly. The U.S. **armed forces** were segregated. Black soldiers could not fight in the same units as white soldiers. They seldom got important jobs in the armed forces. This upset many people. Riots broke out in some cities to demonstrate against the unfair actions toward blacks. Bethune constantly protested against segregation and other racist practices in the armed forces.

One of the colleges where black pilots trained was Tuskegee Institute. These pilots became known as the Tuskegee Airmen. They were successful pilots during World War II.

In 1948, President Harry Truman signed The Women's Armed Services Act. Before this, women could serve in the armed forces only in times of war. The act legalized women serving alongside men in the military during times of peace as well.

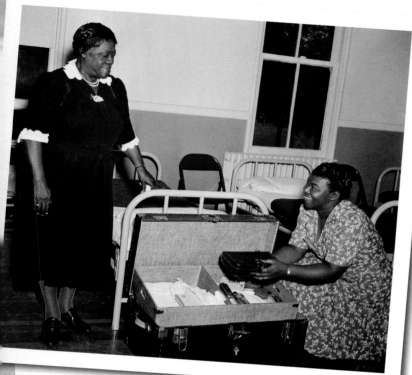

Mary McLeod Bethune welcomed a new member of the Women's Army Corps to her dormitory.

During World War II, women were not allowed to join the armed forces. Instead, they could join other military organizations such as the Women's Army Corps (WAC) or the Army Nurse Corps. However, black women were not allowed to join these organizations right away. Bethune fought to end these racist policies.

Thanks to Bethune's work, black women were finally allowed to serve in the WAC in 1942. Bethune was named a special assistant to the secretary of war. She was responsible for choosing black WAC officer candidates. These women became leaders who helped make important decisions for the corps.

Around this time, Bethune wrote an important essay called "Certain Unalienable Rights." In this essay, she explained that blacks wanted "what the Declaration of Independence and the Constitution and the Bill of Rights say, what the four freedoms establish." In other words, Bethune argued that blacks wanted equality in the eyes of the law.

Bethune (center) stood behind President Truman as he signed into law National Freedom Day in 1948. The day honors the end of slavery.

A group of Bethune-Cookman College students with Mary McLeod Bethune

Chapter Five

A LEGACY OF CIVIL RIGHTS

y the end of World War II, Bethune had already accomplished many things in her life. She was an important force in the world of politics and a respected national leader. She was the first black woman appointed to head a U.S. federal agency. She contributed to significant changes in government. She continued her work in education, believing it was the best way to fight poverty and hardship. She served as a role model for women. She was a loving mother and a successful career woman.

When the war was over, Bethune's hard work caught up with her. She had health problems, and her doctor wanted her to rest. She tried to slow down but was unable to do so. Bethune felt she still had work to do. In 1945, she served as a **consultant** at the conference that led to the United Nations **charter**. President Harry Truman appointed Bethune to a defense committee. She also continued working with Bethune-Cookman College.

Bethune knew she had accomplished a great deal in her life. Yet she also knew there was much more to do. In 1955, at age 79, Bethune wrote a final document titled "My Last Will and Testament." In it she detailed her life goals and gave advice to blacks for the future. She reminded people that "equality for the Negro" had not yet been reached and that they must continue to strive for it. On May 18, 1955, Mary McLeod Bethune died from a heart attack.

Bethune served in advisor roles during the presidencies of Calvin Coolidge and Herbert Hoover. She attended the Child Welfare Conference in 1928 under Coolidge, and the National Commission for Child Welfare during Hoover's presidency. She also advised presidents Roosevelt and Truman.

Mary McLeod Bethune spoke to a crowd at Madison Square Garden in New York City, New York.

In "My Last Will and Testament," Bethune outlined the legacy she wished to leave for fellow blacks. Among the list is "love, hope, a thirst for education, faith, racial dignity, and a desire to live harmoniously with your fellow men."

The year 1955 was important in black history. That December, Rosa Parks, a black woman, was arrested after she refused to give up her bus seat to a white man. People all over the country began to fight similar injustice. They began to protest against discrimination and racism. The battle for civil rights grew stronger than ever.

Mary McLeod Bethune was one of the most influential black women of the twentieth century. She committed her life to uplifting blacks through education, civil rights, and political action. She encouraged black women to reach their full potential.

Today, Bethune is remembered in many ways. Schools are named after her. Her home on the Bethune-Cookman campus is a National Historic Landmark. A bronze statue was erected in 1974 to honor her. It shows Bethune, leaning on her walking cane, passing on her legacy to two children that represent future generations. The statue is located in Lincoln Park in Washington DC.

Mary McLeod Bethune showed that through education and determination, people can achieve their dreams. "Most people think I am a dreamer," she once said. "Through dreams many things have come true."

President Truman (left) honored Mary McLeod Bethune for her contributions to the black community.

Mary McLeod Bethune in front of the
Capitol building in Washington DC, the city
where she accomplished much of her work

TIME LINE

1875
Mary McLeod is born in Mayesville, South Carolina, on July 10.

1885
Mary starts school at Trinity Presbyterian Mission School. In the evenings, she teaches her brothers and sisters what she learned in class.

1890
The "Woman's Era" begins. Black women around the country join clubs and groups to improve their lives and the lives of others.

1894
Mary graduates from Scotia Seminary.

1895
Mary graduates from Moody Bible Institute in Chicago.

1896
The National Association of Colored Women Clubs (NACWC) is founded. Black women around the country join.

1904
Mary McLeod Bethune founds the Daytona Educational and Industrial Training School for Negro Girls in Daytona Beach, Florida.

1923
Bethune's school merges with Cookman Institute of Jacksonville, Florida. It begins as a high school and later becomes a four-year university, Bethune-Cookman University.

1924
Bethune becomes the eighth president of the National Association of Colored Women Clubs (NACWC) and serves until 1928.

1935

The National Association for the Advancement of Colored People (NAACP) awards Bethune the Spingarn Medal. Bethune founds the National Council of Negro Women (NCNW) and begins working with the National Youth Administration (NYA).

1936

Bethune becomes the director of the Division of Negro Affairs of the NYA.

1941

The United States enters World War II. Thousands of black soldiers fight to protect their country throughout the war.

1942

The Women's Army Corps (WAC) begins enlisting women for duties outside combat. Bethune successfully fights the WAC's policy of not accepting black women.

1945

Bethune is a consultant at a conference to draft a United Nations charter.

1955

Bethune's "My Last Will and Testament" is published.

1955

Bethune dies at the age of 79 in her home on the Bethune-Cookman College campus.

1974

Bethune's house on the Bethune-Cookman College campus is named a National Historic Landmark.

GLOSSARY

amendment

(*uh-**mend**-munt*)

An amendment is a change that is made to a law or legal document. The Thirteenth Amendment freed all slaves in the United States.

armed forces

(***armd** for-sez*)

All the groups of a military that protect a nation make up the armed forces. Bethune worked hard to make sure black men were treated fairly in the U.S. armed forces.

charter

(***char**-tur*)

A charter is a formal document that states the duties of a group. Bethune was a consultant at the conference that wrote the United Nations charter.

civil rights

(*siv-il **rites***)

Civil rights are personal freedoms that belong to all U.S. citizens. Bethune worked for the civil rights of blacks to be protected and respected.

consultant

(*kun-**sul**-tunt*)

A consultant is a person who has knowledge in an area and is hired to give advice. President Roosevelt asked Bethune to be a consultant on Negro affairs.

discrimination

(*diss-krim-i-**nay**-shun*)

Discrimination is unfair treatment of people based on differences of race, gender, religion, or culture. Bethune and many other blacks experienced discrimination by whites.

Great Depression

(***grayt** di-**presh**-un*)

The Great Depression was a time of economic crisis in the 1930s. Bethune worked in Negro affairs during the Great Depression.

missionaries

(***mish**-uh-nayr-eez*)

Missionaries are people who teach their religion to others and often work in another country. As a young woman, Bethune wanted to go to Africa as a missionary.

policies

(***pol**-uh-seez*)

Rules and regulations about ways to do something are called policies. Bethune helped President Roosevelt set his policies on race.

potential

(*puh-**ten**-shul*)

Potential is what a person is capable of achieving with his or her talent and intellect. Bethune believed that society did not allow women to reach their full potential.

prejudice

(***prej**-uh-diss*)

Prejudice is a negative feeling or opinion about someone without just cause. Some people felt prejudice against Bethune because she was black.

racism

(***ray**-sih-zum*)

The belief that one race is superior to another is called racism. Bethune and other blacks experienced racism from whites.

scholarship

(***skahl**-ur-ship*)

A sum of money awarded to a student to help pay for her education is called a scholarship. Bethune was given a scholarship to attend Scotia Seminary.

segregation

(*seg-ruh-**gay**-shun*)

Segregation is the act of keeping members of a race, class, or ethnic group apart. Bethune battled segregation laws that were unfair to blacks.

seminary

(***sem**-uh-nayr-ee*)

A seminary is a school that provides religious education. Bethune attended Scotia Seminary as a young girl.

sexism

(***sek**-sizm*)

Sexism is a negative feeling or opinion about someone of the opposite sex. The National Association of Colored Women's Club (NACWC) worked to end sexism against women.

tuition

(*too-**ish**-un*)

Tuition is a fee for going to school. Students paid tuition to attend Bethune-Cookman College.

FURTHER INFORMATION

Books

Bolden, Tonya. *And Not Afraid to Dare*. New York: Scholastic, 2002.

Hansen, Joyce. *African Americans Who Made a Difference*. New York: Scholastic, 2007.

Hermann, Spring. *Struggle for Equality: Women and Minorities in America*. Berkeley Heights, N.J.: Enslow, 2006.

Jones, Victoria Garrett. *Eleanor Roosevelt: A Courageous Spirit*. New York: Sterling, 2007.

Landau, Elaine. *Women's Right to Vote*. New York: Scholastic Library, 2007.

Sharp, Anne Wallace. *Dream Deferred: The Jim Crow Era*. New York: Lucent, 2005.

Videos

Black History: From Civil War Through Today. St. Clair Vision, 2007.

Mary McLeod Bethune: The Spirit of a Champion. Dir. Bill Barnett. History on Video, 2008.

Web Sites

Visit our Web page for links about Mary McLeod Bethune:

http://www.childsworld.com/links

NOTE TO PARENTS, TEACHERS, AND LIBRARIANS: We routinely verify our Web links to make sure they are safe, active sites—so encourage your readers to check them out!

Index